the B.E.E. SERIES

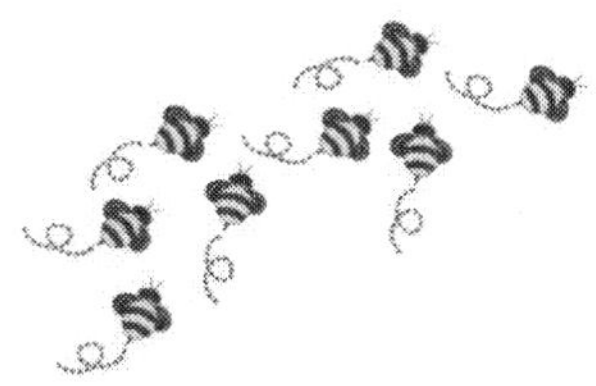

(BELIEVE, EXPECT, ENCOUNTER)

Y.OUR O.WN U.NIQUENESS

*"Let no man despise thy youth;
but be thou an example of the believers, in word,
in conversation, in charity, in spirit, in faith, in purity."
1 Timothy 4:12*

30 Day Devotional Challenge

By: Monya R. Coleman

Believe.**E**xpect.**E**ncounter.**Y**our.**O**wn.**U**niqueness

ISBN: 9781674427010

FOREWORD
ZaMiyah Johnson

As a 14-year old living in this society, there are many opportunities to be what others are trying to be. I am a dancer, cheerleader, gymnast, and an honor roll student. I am a student in a dual-enrollment program where I attend both high school and college. Additionally, I'm very active at my church in dance, youth flag ministry, choir, and the praise and worship ministries. It can all be so extremely challenging.

Sometimes, being a teenager poses a problem for you to fit in. I used to have that problem because everyone saw me as an extra-smart nerdy girl who made straight A's. I was labeled based on my peers' perceptions. I got mad and became very angry, because I could not fit in with any of the groups. I lowered my standards to try to fit in which was a terrible idea. I became distracted and my grades and behavior suffered. I came to my senses and I realized that the very people that I wanted to "fit in with" began to get in mess and fights and I quickly realized that I did not want to be involved.

The Lord and my youth leaders encourage me each week by saying, "ZaMiyah, BEE YOU!" I have to remember who I am and whose I am. I am a child of God! I keep my head held high and continue to pray and believe God to get me through my day as well as my activities. When I keep that mindset, I realize that I have been called by God and I encourage each of you to BEE YOU!

FOREWORD
Karrington Watts

In the life of a 2000's baby, today's society is fun, sad, and psychotic. High school is a confusing stage in life, because of how fast everything comes toward you. You could be the popular kid, the quiet kid that has not caught everything yet, or the kid that just wants to fit in by being like someone else that you clearly are not!

God made you to BEE YOU! Not somebody that you are not! Our generation goes through pain, anxiety, depression, and some bullying that most adults really do not understand. It is because of what is going on in class, home, or in the hallways that makes things so difficult to deal with sometimes. For example, last year I was stressing over how much work I was receiving and the amount of time that I needed to do it by. I knew failure was not an option in any way, so I asked God to help me through it. I started getting more time to where my parents had to tell me what time it was and when to go to sleep. Now, this year, everything is easier even though I have harder classes than last year. But all in all, God helps us through these situations in highly mysterious ways.

All we have to do is trust ourselves these days and trust our Lord and Savior more than ever. You will come back harder than ever. Whatever you are going through, all you have to do is talk about the problems you have. Live life and love life and whatever you do, BEE YOU!

INTRODUCTION

Celebrities, Basketball superstars, Rappers, Personalities, YouTubers, and even Dancers are many of the jobs or careers that our youth are now aspiring to bee. Whereas, these are not bad choices, they are all subject and may not present longevity.

No worries. You can bee whatever you desire to bee. Not only can you bee what you want to but you can also bee who you desire to bee. With that beeing said, it is safe to figure out what your aspirations and inspirations are for your future.

Whatever you choose, I encourage you to BEE Y.O.U.! Bee Your Own Unique self. You are a masterpiece! God broke the mold when He created you. You can outshine the brightest star! Your glow is brighter than the moon's and you bring light to dark situations.

That's right, God outdid Himself when He perfectly designed you. So, in spite of what the world is leaning towards, you can simply choose to bee the best Y.O.U.! My prayer is that you will dig deep within yourself and bee the greatest Y.O.U., you can bee because I am already taken.

So, what does that mean to you? It simply means that you don't have to bee the world-famous singer, because she is already taken. You don't have to bee the GOAT (Greatest Of All Time) on the basketball court, because he may have already been discovered. But you can create your own claim to fame in the Lord as you allow Him to cause you to B.E.E. Y.O.U.!

JESUS JESUS JESUS JESUS JESUS JESUS
JESUS JESUS JESUS JESUS JESUS JESUS
JESUS JESUS JESUS JESUS JESUS JESUS
JESUS JESUS JESUS JESUS JESUS JESUS
JESUS JESUS JESUS JESUS JESUS JESUS
JESUS JESUS JESUS JESUS JESUS JESUS
JESUS JESUS JESUS JESUS JESUS JESUS
JESUS JESUS JESUS JESUS JESUS JESUS
JESUS JESUS JESUS JESUS JESUS JESUS
JESUS JESUS JESUS JESUS JESUS JESUS
JESUS JESUS JESUS JESUS JESUS JESUS
JESUS JESUS JESUS JESUS JESUS JESUS
JESUS JESUS JESUS JESUS JESUS JESUS
JESUS JESUS JESUS JESUS JESUS JESUS
JESUS JESUS JESUS JESUS JESUS JESUS
JESUS JESUS JESUS JESUS JESUS JESUS
JESUS JESUS JESUS JESUS JESUS JESUS
JESUS JESUS JESUS JESUS JESUS JESUS
JESUS JESUS JESUS JESUS JESUS JESUS
JESUS JESUS JESUS JESUS JESUS JESUS
JESUS JESUS JESUS JESUS JESUS JESUS
JESUS JESUS JESUS JESUS JESUS JESUS

because it's ALL ABOUT JESUS!

Dedication

This devotional is dedicated to my teenage Godchildren and God-given children who are in the mix of life in search of how to BEE YOU! To each of you, know that my love for you stems deeper than a feeling, but it is sincerely a heart response for the love of God. My prayer is that each of you will BEE YOU and know that God is in the business of teaching you to walk above the pressure of peers, intimidation, bullying, and other attacks that are familiar to your generation.

To you:
Trinecia DeShae Robinson (NeNe), Ariesus Rashard Preston (AJ), Karrington Christopher Watts (Tut), ZaMiyah Josephine Johnson, JaZarriah Elaintrel Adams, Shamaria Br'Nai Smith, Markaya Bernice Young (Muffin), DeAlonzia Jeanne' Baylor (Dea), Jeremy Ely, Eden Holmes, Jayla Shavone Stewart, Desmond Tyzai Thomas, Ariah Eleece Savannah, Ja'Hiem Lewis, Lynzy Barret (Mae Davis, Sir'Awinn Smith, Kamaria Bevil, Dymond Maleya Wilson, Jaelyn Malae Washington, Kennedy Gayle Anderson, Mikayla Mckenzi Mims, Char'Niyah Rayana Lars, Kelsey Alise Penn, Che'Niya Robinson, , Dreigh'Lyn Robinson, Ty'Kerriyah Robinson, Akima McDade and Ahyala McDade...BEE the BEST YOU that YOU can BEE!

May you each know that you can BEE YOU! Conquer the world and live out loud! Remember the teachings that you have each received and BEE GREAT! The world is waiting on you! Make God proud!

B.E.E. Y.O.U. CHALLENGE

Welcome to the B.E.E. Y.O.U. Challenge. Over the next 30 days, you will be challenged to
Believe, Expect, & Encounter Your Own Uniqueness. This devotional challenge will cause you to dig deeper within and search God for the hidden treasures of your own life.

With each day, you will be immersed into positivity that is guaranteed to strengthen and encourage you. As you progress, you will climb into higher heights and deeper challenges. This journey is going to be unforgettable but must be followed consecutively.

This Alphabetical Guide will further challenge you to B.E.E. the most amazing creature on this side of Heaven. Our world is certainly in need of vessels like you! Take this thirty-day plunge and believe God for the miraculous. We are certain that you will B.E.E. Y.O.U. like no other can be! You are off to an adventurous beginning. Let's finish strong together!

TABLE OF CONTENTS

Day 1:
B.E.E. Awesome, Adventurous, & Accountable

So then, each one of us will give an account of himself to God. Romans 14:12 NASB

There are some pretty awesome and adventurous things to do and bee as a teenager. Of all that you can imagine to do, there is still a need to bee accountable. Beeing accountable speaks to your duty to report, explain, and bee responsible. After all, you are old enough to handle some responsibilities.

For this reason, you must BEE ACCOUNTABLE! Adventure has a way of causing you to lose focus of the time, surroundings, and other necessary issues that are relevant to both your safety and success. Although adventure is exciting, it should never cause you to bee put in harm's way.

Today's Challenge:

BEE AWESOME and experience the breathtaking moments of life. BEE ADVENTUROUS as you discover life's daring moments as a great exploration. BEE Accountable as you take authority and responsibility over your actions; realizing that you are liable.
After you have been all of these things, ask yourself if what you learned caused you to experience, explore, and take responsibility for your own actions? If so, your challenge is complete. If not, try again. Each day a lesson should bee obtained.

Remember, that each of us will give an account of HIMSELF to GOD! What will your explanation bee?

NOTES

(PLEASE JOURNAL YOUR THOUGHTS, FEELINGS, AND PRAYERS ABOUT THIS DEVOTIONAL. BE SURE TO DATE IT.)

Day 2:
B.E.E. Brilliant, Bold & Beneficial

"Everything is permissible," but not everything is beneficial.
"Everything is permissible," but not everything builds up.
I Corinthians 10:23 CSB

You are one brilliant kid! Not only do you possess the mind of Christ to do and bee anything, but you also have His boldness inside of you. That's right, you were created to stand out in the crowd.

By now you should have noticed how so many of your friends and even associates are drawn to you. You normally have the answers to assist in crisis and drama. When decisions are made within your circle, your voice is very notable.

This is an amazing attribute to possess. The truth is, you are a born leader. Having such responsibility challenges you to do what is always beneficial for the entire group. Remember, as a leader, you are beeing followed. Where are you leading them too?

<u>Today's Challenge:</u>

BEE BRILLIANT and show forth the mind of Christ in your decision making, choices, and ability to reason. BEE BOLD and let the world know that you are unashamed of the gospel of Jesus Christ. BEE BENEFICIAL to all you encounter and ensure that the value you add to a situation is invaluable.
I challenge you to bee brilliant and shine bright. I further challenge you to bee bold today and take charge in Jesus' name. Finally, I challenge you to bee beneficial and helpful in every situation.

Remember, that all things are permissible (anything goes in the world), but not all things are beneficial (good for you)!

NOTES

(PLEASE JOURNAL YOUR THOUGHTS, FEELINGS, AND PRAYERS ABOUT THIS DEVOTIONAL. BE SURE TO DATE IT.)

Day 3:
B.E.E. Caring, Clever & Confident

And this is the confidence that we have in him, that, if we ask anything according to his will, he heareth us: I John 5:14 KJV

In today's society, Millennials are the carriers of our future. That's right, the ball has been given to you on your court. The next move is up to you on how to win the game called life.

Many of you have the gentle attribute to BEE CARING and show the love of God. Others within your peer group are extremely clever and techno-savvy. This too is a great quality to possess. Although beeing caring and CLEVER are essential characteristics to hold, you must BEE CONFIDENT in how you display these features.

Bee confident that you are doing great feats in the name of the Lord Jesus. Bee caring enough to lend a helping hand and bee clever enough to understand where you are in the Lord, because He is deeply concerned about you!

Today's Challenge:

BEE Caring, Clever, & Confident in the Lord Jesus Christ! He is your only hope for life. You can and you will make greater moves in Him, but you must understand that your confidence must bee solely resting in Him!

Remember: Godly confidence is hottest, because Godly confidence is modest!

NOTES

(PLEASE JOURNAL YOUR THOUGHTS, FEELINGS, AND PRAYERS ABOUT THIS DEVOTIONAL. BE SURE TO DATE IT.)

Day 4:
B.E.E. Decent, Delightful, & Devoted

Let your heart therefore be wholly devoted to the LORD our God, to walk in His statues and to keep His commandments, as at this day.
I Kings 8:61 NASB

Decency may be a lost standard required by the world, but not for our God. He commands each of us to BEE DECENT and appropriate in all that we endeavor to do. This is such a DELIGHTFUL task, because beeing decent causes you to respect yourself as well as know your worth.

As you discover your worth, you should embrace the delightful aspects of the Lord and how He is devoted to you and your well-beeing. He has your best interest at heart and He desires that you show Him equal devotion.

BEE DEVOTED to the most faithful person you will ever meet….Jesus! He is capable of beeing your best friend, confidant, and advisor. He is devoted to giving you the best and desires nothing less than you living your BEST LIFE!

Today's Challenge:

BEE Decent in your dealings and delightful in your approach. Those who are devoted with their whole heart will always walk with the Lord.

Remember: Those who are devoted will always triumph, because they are committed to an Almighty God!

NOTES

(PLEASE JOURNAL YOUR THOUGHTS, FEELINGS, AND PRAYERS ABOUT THIS DEVOTIONAL. BE SURE TO DATE IT.)

Day 5:
B.E.E. Educated & Extraordinary

O God, your deeds are extraordinary! What god can compare to our great God? Psalm 77:13 NET

Is there any profession in today's society that does not require you to bee educated? There are very few that we can call to mind in an effort to bee successful. For this reason, you are beeing encouraged to bee academically proficient as you progress towards your future.

God is not intimidated by your ability to BEE EDUCATED; in fact He welcomes your ability to become knowledgeable. God does indeed want to make you to BEE an EXTRAORDINARY creature. Because He has such an extraordinary future ahead for you, He is rooting you on daily.

Whatever you decide, make your choice wisely. Beeing educated can catapult you in places you could never imagine. Beeing educated and loving the ONLY WISE GOD will cause you to live an extraordinary life that is designed for His glory!

<u>Today's Challenge:</u>

BEE Educated and watch God excel you to places you could only envision in Him. BEE Extraordinary in your endeavors and never settle for the common. I challenge you to BEE Excellent in your Educational quest as well as BEE Extraordinary in your efforts!

Remember, our God is extraordinary in all His ways. He desires to "do it BIG" in your life! Will you let Him?

NOTES

(PLEASE JOURNAL YOUR THOUGHTS, FEELINGS, AND PRAYERS ABOUT THIS DEVOTIONAL. BE SURE TO DATE IT.)

Day 6:
B.E.E. Friendly & Faithful

A faithful man shall abound with blessings:
Proverbs 28:20a KJV

Friends are priceless gifts of God that have been given to each of us as an extension of His love. The Bible suggests that in order to have friends, you must BEE FRIENDLY. If you are one with a plethora of friends, you are blessed.

Having friends is a great indication that you have the ability to bee a friend. The greatest gift of that bond lies in the ability to BEE FAITHFUL. Having friends is always good, but having faithful friends is priceless.

Faithful friends always let you know that they can bee depended on whenever they are needed. Not only can you trust them with your secrets, but they are faithfully committed to you and keep your best interest at heart. Bee the faithful friend that you desire and entrust God with your friendships. Afterall, we are friends of God!

<u>Today's Challenge:</u>

BEE Friendly and Faithful to those you encounter along your journey! I challenge you to learn how to bee a committed friend who is faithful in their endeavors and pursuit of life in Christ.

Remember, we are friends of the Lord and He is faithful!

NOTES

(PLEASE JOURNAL YOUR THOUGHTS, FEELINGS, AND PRAYERS ABOUT THIS DEVOTIONAL. BE SURE TO DATE IT.)

Day 7:
B.E.E. Goal-oriented & Great

Commit your works to the LORD, and your plans will be established.
Proverbs 16:3 NET

BEEING GOAL-ORIENTED can bee extremely hard, because there are so many options in life. Whatever you choose to do, your plan can always bee successful if goals are guiding your decisions. Beeing goal-oriented serves as an outline for greatness.

No ifs, ands, or buts about it… you can BEE GREAT! Whether you plan its course or stumble upon it, greatness comes with preparation. It is noted that some of the most successful people in the world are goal-oriented.

Today, you can choose to BEE GREAT simply by learning how to BEE GOAL-ORIENTED! The process of planning and achieving such goals will lead to success.

<u>Today's Challenge:</u>
I challenge you to bee goal-oriented. Write your five-year short term goals. Write the details of how you plan to achieve the goal(s) and what it will take to attain such success.

Remember, beeing goal-oriented will cause you to bee great! We can plan to succeed or plan to fail!

NOTES

(PLEASE JOURNAL YOUR THOUGHTS, FEELINGS, AND PRAYERS ABOUT THIS DEVOTIONAL. BE SURE TO DATE IT.)

Day 8:
B.E.E. Happy & Healthy

Happy are the people with such blessings. Happy are the people whose God is the Lord. Psalm 144:15 CSB

BEE Happy! In life there are many instances that can make us happy. Whether your happiness is found when your favorite sports team wins the game or in receiving an unexpected gift; it feels good to bee happy.

To BEE HAPPY assists with your position to BEE HEALTHY! We have heard "don't worry, bee happy!" That is a powerful attitude to have in life. The happier you become, the healthier you will act. A happy mind is a healthy mind.

Today, bee sharp enough to seek out happiness daily. Bee healthy enough to understand that your happiness is needed to remain healthy. Find your happiness in the Lord and spread it to as many friends and friendemies as you encounter. Happy is contagious.

<u>Today's Challenge:</u>

BEE Happy and look to spread the positive news of what is happening. BEE Healthy and understand that healthy people are much happier people. Allow God to show you how effective you can bee as you spread His happiness and show others how to bee healthy. Each day a lesson should bee obtained.

Remember, don't worry, BEE Happy & Healthy!

NOTES

(PLEASE JOURNAL YOUR THOUGHTS, FEELINGS, AND PRAYERS ABOUT THIS DEVOTIONAL. BE SURE TO DATE IT.)

Day 9:
B.E.E. Intentional & Initiate

Having, therefore, brethren, boldness for the entrance into the holy places, in the blood of Jesus, which way he did initiate for us.
Hebrews 10:19-21 YLT

BEE INTENTIONAL in everything that you do for the Lord! Your deliberate attempts to live out loud and please Him will never go unnoticed. You must realize that you can start the ball to rolling more when your motives have purpose.

You can INITIATE boldness, friendships, and holiness. Bee intentional as you show others how to establish and take responsibility for the their actions. You have been called to start fires that will ignite and cause others to blaze for Jesus!

<u>Today's Challenge:</u>

BEE Intentional and allow your actions to prove that you can bee trusted. BEE one who Initiates as you redefine life's meaning and discover your God-given purpose. As you progress in the journey of life, I challenge you to become a trailblazer who clears paths for others to follow. Your Intentional Initiative will bee remembered for years to come.

Remember, only Intentionality is recognized after it is Initiated!!!

NOTES

(PLEASE JOURNAL YOUR THOUGHTS, FEELINGS, AND PRAYERS ABOUT THIS DEVOTIONAL. BE SURE TO DATE IT.)

Day 10:
B.E.E. JUST LIKE JESUS

In your lives you must think and act like Christ Jesus.
Philippians 2:5-11 NCV

BEE JUST LIKE JESUS! Wow! That has to bee the hardest thing ever. Afterall, how is that even possible? Who could bee just like Jesus?
I am certain that as you turned to this very page, you somehow felt overwhelmed. Beeing told to bee like Jesus should not bee as hard as it is presented to bee.

The best explanation is to find out His character. In order to bee like Him, we must realize that He was a human just like each of us. He knew of those who probably annoyed Him, yet~~,~~ He was kind and loving. He knew no sin and He lived an upright life, yet~~,~~ He was tempted like others.

Find a way in your actions and deeds to BEE just like JESUS. Rather than reading this from a literary perspective, BEE just like Jesus was and is. Bee forgiving, and most importantly~~,~~ Bee like Jesus as you walk in obedience. Jesus was obedient even to the cross.

<u>Today's Challenge:</u>
BEE just like Jesus… in words, actions, and deeds!

Remember: To imitate Christ is to know Him!

NOTES

(PLEASE JOURNAL YOUR THOUGHTS, FEELINGS, AND PRAYERS ABOUT THIS DEVOTIONAL. BE SURE TO DATE IT.)

Day 11:
B.E.E. Keen & Key

Keen insight wins favor, but the conduct of the unfaithful is harsh.
Proverbs 13:15 NET

BEE KEEN! Your sharpness is needed to know what is of God and what is not. Dullness can cause you to bee fooled and miss things that are key.

Because of this, you must BEE KEY in your reasoning, decision making, and your responses. How can you bee keen and key? It is easier than you think. Trust God in all that you do. He will give you keen discernment (insight) and key information that will explain the questions of life.

Bee keen and realize you are God's key player. He is depending on you to trust Him for all of life's problems. When you prove that you are in faith, you can have full assurance that He will answer His children.

<u>Today's Challenge:</u>

I challenge you to have sharp faith in your God. Bee Keen enough to seek Him in all things as well as for all things. After you discover your dependence on Him, you can Bee the Key for others to unlock His goodness.

Remember, Bee Keen and Bee the Key! Your insight will unlock worlds of favorable riches!

NOTES

(PLEASE JOURNAL YOUR THOUGHTS, FEELINGS, AND PRAYERS ABOUT THIS DEVOTIONAL. BE SURE TO DATE IT.)

Day 12:
B.E.E. Loyal & Loved

He who pursues righteousness and loyalty finds life, righteousness and honor. Proverbs 21:21 NASB

Loyalty is never-ending. Just like the love God has for His children, loyalty causes you to understand that you are loved. Wow! What a privileged statement.

How awesome to know that we have been selected to BEE LOYAL just like our Father. Loyalty should never bee conditional or based on circumstances. We should consider how Jesus loves each of us. He does not have stipulations on His love. He simply tells us to BEE LOVED.

Today, bee loyal to those who you love.

<u>Today's Challenge:</u>

I challenge you to examine how loyal you have been to your family and friends. After doing so, re-examine your motives and make sure that your loyalty was prompted by love. If this is the case, you are well on you way to a life of loyalty and love.

Remember, loyalty should be eternal; just like God's love!

NOTES

(PLEASE JOURNAL YOUR THOUGHTS, FEELINGS, AND PRAYERS ABOUT THIS DEVOTIONAL. BE SURE TO DATE IT.)

Day 13:
B.E.E. Motivated & Mature

Brethren, do not be children in your thinking; yet in evil be infants, but in your thinking be mature. I Corinthians 14:20 NASB

You are still so young. Is it time for you to mature? Day by day you are developing into a more mature beeing. Not only are you developing, but you are growing. As your body is changing, your mind, attitude, and outlook are BEEING MOTIVATED to shift as well.

As you are progressing into the next levels of life, you are encouraged to BEE MATURE. Games you played as a five-year old, you normally don't play as a teenager. This is not because you cannot play them, but the normal mindset is that "you are too old to bee doing that!"

Today, Bee Motivated to Bee Mature in the Lord. He has entrusted you to tell others about His greatness. You are mature enough to give your testimony and tell what God has done and been to you.

<u>Today's Challenge:</u>

Bee Motivated to Bee Mature! When situations arise that you know are beneath you, bee mature and trust God for deliverance. You are old enough and they (your friends) are watching you!

Remember, Make God Proud!

NOTES

(PLEASE JOURNAL YOUR THOUGHTS, FEELINGS, AND PRAYERS ABOUT THIS DEVOTIONAL. BE SURE TO DATE IT.)

Day 14:
B.E.E. Noticeable

Keep your eyes open, hold tight to your convictions, give it all you've got, be resolute, and love without stopping.
I Corinthians 16:13-14 MSG

BEE NOTICEABLE! Stand out! You have been equipped with such great faith and the world needs to see it! That's right, live out loud! You can no longer bee silent!

While at the football game, fans are the first ones noted, because they are dressed in their team attire. They are normally the loudest in the stands, and those who are die-hard fans are completely dedicated to their team. You don't have to beg them to cheer; their love for the team is noticeable.

Today and everyday that follows, your faith can BEE NOTICEABLE! If you are a fan of your God, open your mouth and let others know. Make noise and declare His excellent greatness! Shout to the Lord and thank Him for protection! As you speak of Him, others will take notice that you are not ashamed of the Gospel or your God! Just like the hype that takes place in the stands, your cheer to your God will spread as the crowd goes wild!

<u>Today's Challenge:</u>
I challenge you to BEE NOTICEABLE in your FAITH! This does not mean you beat others down with the Bible. It does mean that they will notice that there is something "positively different" about you.

Remember, your Faith is beeing noticed!

NOTES

(PLEASE JOURNAL YOUR THOUGHTS, FEELINGS, AND PRAYERS ABOUT THIS DEVOTIONAL. BE SURE TO DATE IT.)

Day 15:
B.E.E. Outstanding & Obedient

So then, dear brothers and sisters, be firm. Do not be moved! Always be outstanding in the work of the Lord, knowing that your labor is not in vain in the Lord. I Corinthians 15:58 NET

You may or may not have been encouraged to BEE OUTSTANDING in life. This can seem as if great pressure is beeing placed on you. The truth is, you are already one outstanding kid! That's the way our Daddy God sees us.
He says, "you are the apple of His eye!" If it were possible, your picture would bee on Heaven's refrigerator. The Lord thinks the world of you!

When you are chosen to BEE OBEDIENT, your extraordinary gifts stand out the more. Not only are you God's favorite, but everyone else begins to see His glory on your life. It is true that your obedience to the Lord causes you to outshine most. So today, continue to do just that… Bee Outstanding as you continue to Bee Obedient!

<u>Today's Challenge:</u>

BEE OBEDIENT to parents, teachers, elders, and well-meaning friends. Your obedience will cause you to walk in favor and bee considered as an outstanding individual!

Remember, to BEE OUTSTANDING, most will notice if you can first BEE OBEDIENT!

NOTES

(PLEASE JOURNAL YOUR THOUGHTS, FEELINGS, AND PRAYERS ABOUT THIS DEVOTIONAL. BE SURE TO DATE IT.)

Day 16:
B.E.E. Persistent

I pursue as my goal the prize promised by God's heavenly call in Christ Jesus. Philippians 3:14 HCSB

Have you ever constantly repeated doing something; good or bad? If you have done so, you have proven to BEE PERSISTENT! Although this seems like such a big word, it represents your ability to continue in doing something.

Maybe you have been persistent in making good grades. If you have, you can rest assured that your hard work will pay off resulting in a great college experience and career. You may have been persistent in giving your best care and concern at home. You have proven that you can bee persistently responsible.

Understand that persistence will reproduce the prize that God has promised to each of you. It is when you trust Him in your pursuit, that your efforts will become more devoted. You will see godly results as you: set goals, stay true and dedicated, and conquer what you began as you prove your persistence.

Today's Challenge:

BEE PERSISTENT in word and deed. Whatever you do, persevere until you see the desired results. The prize is always better than the price paid.

Remember, Persistent Faith produces Persistent Results!

NOTES

(PLEASE JOURNAL YOUR THOUGHTS, FEELINGS, AND PRAYERS ABOUT THIS DEVOTIONAL. BE SURE TO DATE IT.)

Day 17:
B.E.E. Qualified

Giving thanks to the Father, who has qualified us to share in the inheritance of the saints (God's people) in the Light.
Colossians 1:12 AMP

Are you qualified? For what you might ask? My answer would bee "yes, you are called to BEE QUALIFIED for everything!" It is not what makes you qualified, but more so who has qualified you.

JESUS! He is the Man with the plan. He is the one who has called us from darkness into the marvelous Light. His calling has qualified us for His greater works.

Today, bee qualified and know that your competence is NOT based on anything you can do or have done. Jesus suggested that you BEE QUALIFIED by the work He has done for you!

<u>Today's Challenge:</u>
Recognize what you have been qualified for and get busy with your tasks.

Remember, you have already been counted worthy because Jesus has called you to BEE QUALIFIED!

NOTES

(PLEASE JOURNAL YOUR THOUGHTS, FEELINGS, AND PRAYERS ABOUT THIS DEVOTIONAL. BE SURE TO DATE IT.)

Day 18:
B.E.E. Radiant

Those who look to Him are radiant with joy; their faces will never be ashamed. Psalm 34:5 HCSB

Shine bright like a diamond! Your glow is ever so light and God has called you to BEE RADIANT! Everyone is beaming in on you, because you are like glow-in-the-dark beads. You never stop shining.

To Bee Radiant, you must realize what is causing you to glisten. If your answer is Jesus, I can assure you that this glow is eternal. He causes the illumination for all to see His glory.

Today, bee radiant and allow His glare to bee seen in the joy you possess. Know that you are radiant and your brilliance in Christ can not become dim. His love alone is enough to create an everlasting luster and radiance.

<u>Today's Challenge:</u>

As you shine in your radiance, know who you are shining for. If at any time you feel like your glare is your own, you may instantly become dull! Keep Jesus first and you will bee radiant!

Remember, SHINE!

NOTES

(PLEASE JOURNAL YOUR THOUGHTS, FEELINGS, AND PRAYERS ABOUT THIS DEVOTIONAL. BE SURE TO DATE IT.)

Day 19:
B.E.E. Sufficient

Not that we are sufficient of ourselves to think any thing as of ourselves; but our sufficiency is of God; II Corinthians 3:5 KJV

BEE SUFFICIENT in everything that you do! If you are able to commit to that command then you must bee aware of what it means to bee sufficient. If you are unsure, you have an opportunity of a lifetime as you learn to trust God.

Beeing sufficient speaks to you having enough of what is needed. There is only one way to ensure that to bee so, and that is by putting your trust and confidence in Jesus. He is enough! Your Father owns and rules everything and He has given that same authority to you.

Today, bee sufficient and know that Jesus does not desire for us to live in lack. He is the God of all sufficiency. There is no lack in Jesus. Having faith in Him is like having an ATM card that never runs out of money. You have access to use it for what you need as well as what you want for the rest of your life. Trust Him as He continues to make you to bee sufficient.

<u>Today's Challenge:</u>

BEE Sufficient in your trust of the Father. He desires to bee your sufficiency.

Remember, God is ALL sufficient! Your sufficiency rests in Him. Whatever you need, God's got it! Look for "it" in Jesus!

NOTES

(PLEASE JOURNAL YOUR THOUGHTS, FEELINGS, AND PRAYERS ABOUT THIS DEVOTIONAL. BE SURE TO DATE IT.)

Day 20:
B.E.E. Talented

Each of you as a good manager must use the gift (talents) that God has given you to serve others. I Peter 4:10 GWT

Talented by definition is the God-given ability to do what you do using unique skills. These skills are not learned, because they are given by God. They are already a part of your genetic makeup in which God has given them for you to use for His glory! He wants you to BEE TALENTED!

Whether your talent is singing, dancing, playing sports, or serving others, you possess this gift to serve others. That's right; your gift was never given to make you popular but more or less to make God famous. If you spend your time doing this, He is sure to exalt your talents for all men to see.

Today, serve others with your talents. You can bee talented and show forth His glory as you use your talents to the best of your ability.

<u>Today's Challenge:</u>

Remember, beeing talented is a privilege that many never tap into, because they use the gift for their own glory. Use all that you have been given to bring honor to His name.

NOTES

(PLEASE JOURNAL YOUR THOUGHTS, FEELINGS, AND PRAYERS ABOUT THIS DEVOTIONAL. BE SURE TO DATE IT.)

Day 21:
B.E.E. Unique, Unafraid, & Unstoppable

The Lord himself will lead you and be with you. He will not fail you or abandon you, so do not lose courage or be afraid.
Deuteronomy 31:8 GNT

You were created to BEE UNIQUE in everything that you do! That was the initial plan of the Father as He fashioned you in His image. You were uniquely made and not like anyone else, because you were fearfully and wonderfully made. Therefore, you do not have to live in fear.

You can BEE UNAFRAID, because the Father is entrusting you with His boldness. You must go out of your way and bee who God has called you to bee. No apologies needed. You are required to bee unafraid in your endeavors, because God is ALWAYS with you. He wants you to remember He will never leave or forsake you as you are on your journey to become unstoppable.

Today, BEE UNSTOPPABLE! Go hard for what you believe and fight for the cause of Christ. If you have a God-given mission, bee unstoppable in your pursuit. Many people will be inspired by your ability to stand out, ~~and~~ bee unique, and unafraid; to know that in God, you are unstoppable.

<u>Today's Challenge:</u>

BEE Unique, Unafraid, & Unstoppable in everything you do, so that God will know that He can use you!

Remember, You are Unique! You are Unafraid! You are Unstoppable!

NOTES

(PLEASE JOURNAL YOUR THOUGHTS, FEELINGS, AND PRAYERS ABOUT THIS DEVOTIONAL. BE SURE TO DATE IT.)

Day 22:
B.E.E. VICTORIOUS & A VISIONARY

But thanks be to God, who gives us the victory {as conquerors} through our Lord Jesus Christ. I Corinthians 15:57 AMP

No matter what battle, competition, or race is taking place; every participant wants to win. Winning causes us to feel as if we are victors. God does not want us to just feel like victors, He wants us to BEE VICTORIOUS and see your vision manifest before your very eyes.

In order to see the unfolding take place, you must BEE A VISIONARY! You have to gain insight that you are already walking victoriously over every obstacle life throws. You also have to realize that in the game of life, you have to possess a winner's mentality. Once you see yourself in it, you can achieve beeing victorious.

Today, bee a visionary and see yourself as victorious. If you don't, others wont! Know that in God, all we do is win!

Today's Challenge:

BEE Victorious and know that you have been built for this. If God brings you to it, He will bring your through it!

Remember, See the vision and walk in victory!

NOTES

(PLEASE JOURNAL YOUR THOUGHTS, FEELINGS, AND PRAYERS ABOUT THIS DEVOTIONAL. BE SURE TO DATE IT.)

Day 23:
B.E.E. Wise & Willing

The wise hear them and grow in wisdom; those with understanding gain guidance. Proverbs 1:5 CEB

Life offers many opportunities for decisions that must bee made. If you are to bee victorious, you must BEE WISE. Beeing wise causes you to trust in the power of God to properly judge and discern what is true, right, and has the best outcome. You can not just have wisdom, you must bee willing to use it for the greatest conclusion.

You must BEE WILLING to believe God in every situation. This is the only way to your prosperity in the Lord. Get focused and know that your willingness creates obedience. Once you are in complete submission to the Lord, you will bee considered wise.

Today, bee wise enough to seek the Lord and willing to obey. You will bee glad that you did. Others will benefit from both your wisdom and your willingness to bring honor to your King.

<u>Today's Challenge:</u>

BEE mindful of what you are thinking about and your actions that are constantly on display in the lives of others.

Remember, the wise are always willing!

NOTES
(PLEASE JOURNAL YOUR THOUGHTS, FEELINGS, AND PRAYERS ABOUT THIS DEVOTIONAL. BE SURE TO DATE IT.)

Day 24:
B.E.E. eXuberant

At that, Jesus rejoiced, exuberant in the Holy Spirit. "I thank you, Father…" Luke 10:2a MSG

There is a lot going on in life. If you get caught up in looking at what you see, you will bee greatly distracted. No matter what is going on or wrong, you can find complete joy in Jesus and BEE EXUBERANT.

To bee exuberant speaks to your joyful enthusiasm in the Lord! This is no ordinary happiness, but this excitement overflows. How do you get to rejoice in a day like this? It can only bee done in the Lord.

Today, bee exuberant in your faith in the Father. The Lord loves a cheerful giver and a joyful heart. No matter the dullness the world is presenting, you can have enthusiasm in serving God.

Today's Challenge:

BEE Exuberant and give God all the glory in all that you do for the sake of the Lord!

Remember, the joy of the Lord is your strength! Bee exuberant and remain full of joy.

NOTES

(PLEASE JOURNAL YOUR THOUGHTS, FEELINGS, AND PRAYERS ABOUT THIS DEVOTIONAL. BE SURE TO DATE IT.)

Day 25:
B.E.E. YOUTHFUL

Let no one look down on [you because of] your youth, but be an example and set a pattern for the believers in speech, in conduct, in love, in faith, and in [moral] purity. I Timothy 4:12 AMP

You are one amazing kid! You can do any and everything you put your mind to do! Do not ever conform to any idol word that discourages you from beeing the absolute best you can bee! In this, you have been charged to BEE YOUTHFUL!

Beeing youthful is what you have to do. No matter your age, you must keep a youthful heart and strive for excellence. You can make a mark on society in your faith, actions, and your love for the Master!

Today, bee youthful and never lose your ability to have child-like faith. Believe the unbelievable! Achieve the unachievable! Soar and reach higher heights in your faith. Whatever you do, bee youthful!

<u>Today's Challenge:</u>
BEE Youthful and enjoy your life!

Remember, your youthfulness should never fade!

NOTES

(PLEASE JOURNAL YOUR THOUGHTS, FEELINGS, AND PRAYERS ABOUT THIS DEVOTIONAL. BE SURE TO DATE IT.)

Day 26:
B.E.E. Zealous

Those whom I love, I reprove and discipline, so be zealous and repent. Revelation 3:19 ESV

There is an enthusiastic devotion that has been released in the earth realm to God's people. You have been set up to prosper and God is waiting to use you for His glory. I encourage you to BEE ZEALOUS!

Beeing zealous suggests that you keep an excitement about loving God and His people. You are loved and must remember the price that was paid for your very existence. Never give up or leave your happy place in the Lord.

Today, bee zealous and always bee ready to serve and bless God! Give more than 100% in your every endeavor. Go out of your way to give, love, and serve. When you stand before the Father, He will honor you for beeing zealous!

<u>Today's Challenge:</u>
BEE Zealous and keep the fire of God lit in your life. Do not allow anyone to extinguish your fire or cause you to simmer. Stay Lit!

Remember, God loves a pure zeal!

NOTES

(PLEASE JOURNAL YOUR THOUGHTS, FEELINGS, AND PRAYERS ABOUT THIS DEVOTIONAL. BE SURE TO DATE IT.)

Day 27:
B.E.E. WHO GOD CALLED YOU TO BEE

Nevertheless, as the Lord has assigned to each one, as God has called each person, so must he live. I give this sort of direction in all the churches. I Corinthians 7:17 NET

Today, BEE WHO GOD CALLED YOU TO BEE! Write your thoughts, prayers, and concerns about what that is. Meditate (study over and over) on what you believe it is and share with your parents, youth leaders, or trusted friends.

NOTES

(PLEASE JOURNAL YOUR THOUGHTS, FEELINGS, AND PRAYERS ABOUT THIS DEVOTIONAL. BE SURE TO DATE IT.)

Day 28:
B.E.E. ALL THAT YOU CAN TO BEE

And in all things show yourself to be an example of good works, with purity in doctrine [having the strictest regard for integrity and truth], dignified, Titus 2:7 AMP

Today, BEE ALL THAT YOU CAN TO BEE! Write your thoughts, prayers, and concerns about what that is. Meditate (study over and over) on what you believe it is and share with your parents, youth leaders, or trusted friends.

NOTES

(PLEASE JOURNAL YOUR THOUGHTS, FEELINGS, AND PRAYERS ABOUT THIS DEVOTIONAL. BE SURE TO DATE IT.)

Day 29:
B.E.E. MORE THAN YOU COULD TO BEE

Study and do your best to present yourself to God approved,
II Timothy 2:15 AMP

Today, BEE MORE THAN YOU COULD BEE! Write your thoughts, prayers, and concerns about what that is. Meditate (study over and over) on what you believe it is and share with your parents, youth leaders, or trusted friends.

NOTES

(PLEASE JOURNAL YOUR THOUGHTS, FEELINGS, AND PRAYERS ABOUT THIS DEVOTIONAL. BE SURE TO DATE IT.)

Day 30:
B.E.E. WHAT YOU WANT TO BEE

I can do all things through Christ which strengtheneth me.
Philippians 4:13 KJV

Today, BEE WHAT YOU WANT TO BEE! Write your thoughts, prayers, and concerns about what that is. Meditate (study over and over) on what you believe it is and share with your parents, youth leaders, or trusted friends.

NOTES
(PLEASE JOURNAL YOUR THOUGHTS, FEELINGS, AND PRAYERS ABOUT THIS DEVOTIONAL. BE SURE TO DATE IT.)

APPEAL TO CHRIST

No greater example of love has been witnessed in all the world than God's manifested love for His Son, Jesus Christ. The Gospel message in summation rests on these words: "But God demonstrates His own love toward us, in that while we were still sinners, Christ died for us" (Romans 5:8).

Knowing this great news gives the unbeliever, backslider, and Saint hope that they are NOT too far for God's arm to reach them at the point in which they stand.

My personal appeal to you the reader is that you need a Savior! We all do! If indeed you have not made Jesus Lord over your life, my plea is that you can receive Him today by following this simple, yet powerful statement and prayer.

ABC's of the Gospel: Admit, Believe, Confess
"But what saith it? The word is nigh thee, even in thy mouth, and in thy heart: that is, the word of faith, which we preach; That if thou shalt confess with thy mouth the Lord Jesus, and shalt believe in thine heart that God hath raised him (Jesus) from the dead, thou shalt be saved." Romans 10:8-9 KJV

Admit that you are a sinner and in need of a Savior.

Believe that Jesus is the Son of God who knew no sin, yet He gave His life as a ransom for our sin. Believe in the Lord Jesus and you shall be saved (Acts 16:31).

Confess with your mouth as you invite Jesus to live in your heart that JESUS IS LORD!
If you have followed through, my prayer is that you are saved! Welcome to the Body of Christ! You have a vital part and we need you to survive. For this reason, I pray you will allow the Lord to lead you to a church where you are able to submit to leadership and serve in a capacity that brings God glory!
In Jesus' name, we thank Him for YOU!
#YouAreWorthFightingFor #Romans1:16

ABOUT THE AUTHOR

Monya Laraine Robinson Coleman is a native of Shreveport, Louisiana and has been passionate about writing since childhood. She completely feels the pains that the youth endure and hopes to bring them to a place of understanding what it means to BEE YOU. Monya desires to see them delivered and walking in their own uniqueness.

Monya enjoys being a student of God's word, hanging out with the youth and certainly hosting events that will minister to the youth. As she continues to pursue excellence in the Lord, you can look for more upcoming projects, events, and other avenues for the Lord to reveal His glory.

To God BEE ALL the Glory!

Monya R. Coleman

Made in the USA
Columbia, SC
30 May 2025